RUSSIA, ANYONE?

A Completely
Uncalled-for History
of the U.S.S.R.

Books by Eric Nicol and Peter Whalley

RUSSIA, ANYONE?

SAY, UNCLE

AN UNINHIBITED HISTORY OF CANADA

HARPER & ROW, Publishers
New York, Evanston, and London

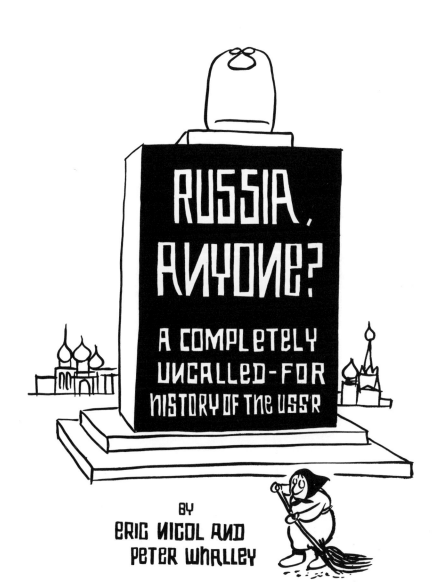

RUSSIA, ANYONE?

A COMPLETELY UNCALLED-FOR HISTORY OF THE USSR

BY
ERIC NICOL AND
PETER WHALLEY

FIRST EDITION

LIBRARY OF CONGRESS CATALOG CARD NUMBER: 63–16513

Note

Any resemblance between this history of Russia and any other history of Russia is coincidental. All historical persons mentioned are fictional, including Joseph Stalin and Nikita Khrushchev. Where it has been necessary to refer to real persons (e.g., Donald Duck), the names have been changed, except those of the authors which were already fictitious.

Acknowledgments

In preparing the material for this book the authors received assistance and encouragement from nobody. Least of all their wives. From the Rockefeller Foundation of New York they got short shrift. They are grateful to Miss Irina Blavitz for typing the manuscript but understood that she would bring back the typewriter.

The work took the authors two years to complete, divided into one month of actual writing and twenty-three months of bickering over how the royalties should be split.

Introduction (Formal)

Here we go gathering
nyets in May . . .
—old UN folk song

WITH THEIR BOOK *Say, Uncle* NICOL AND WHALLEY DID for the history of the United States what the French Revolution did for Louis XVI, namely abridged it and made any further history unnecessary. The publisher has felt that the authors can do no less for Russia, especially if he hopes to get a Christmas card from the FBI. Hence this sequel in which our historians prove that it was not luck alone that determined the success of their initial soaring to new heights of ineptitude.

Indeed, their history of the U.S. was flawed here and there by facts, colored by accuracies that somehow detracted from the work as a whole. No such blemishes appear in this present work, thanks to the *total ignorance* which the authors were able to bring to their study of Russia. The material has been carefully screened to

7

eliminate any statement not solidly based on personal fancies, prejudice, hearsay and old wives' tales (names of old wives consulted will be mailed, on request, in a plain brown wrapper).

Their sketchy acquaintance with Russian history has also enabled the authors to examine more thoroughly than otherwise Russian theater, art, literature and sports, including some pretty definitive notes linking the men's high jump with Russia's space program.

They also provide documented answers to questions that have long troubled the so-called experts on Russia. For instance:

Was Lenin pro-Communist?

Has Russia felt unloved, and if so why?

Why do Russian hockey players look so lumpy?

Did Stalin smoke in bed?

Does the Russian spy system depend on sex or vice versa?

Russian soldiers walk along the street hand in hand, little fingers interlaced. Is this sinister? (See chapter headed "Linky-Pinky Hanky-Panky.")

These and many other previously puzzling mysteries are scrutinized in this volume, which also establishes that, historically, Russia is older than believed though not half as old as she looks.

Introduction (Formal)

Such are only a few of the gaps in knowledge plugged by this study of Russia, which is not only overdue but presumed lost. As a text it is expected to be particularly welcome to teachers, being light enough to reach students in the back row if thrown with a sharp wrist break.

This is the only history of Russia chosen to be given away inside every new washing machine of a well-known make . . . because it brainwashes gently, is kind to even the daintiest notions.

A NOTE ON METHOD

Winston Churchill has described Russia as "a mystery wrapped in an enigma." In other words, Russia has been sold as a package. And as with every package, the problem is: Where do you get your thumbnail under the cellophane?

This is where most histories of Russia get off to a bad start, fumbling around and often opening the thing upside down. To avoid this common error the authors have adopted the method suggested by Toynbee.* This is to take Russian history in the middle and work both ways at once, the one who reaches the end first to cry "Bingo!"

* Fred Toynbee, Whalley's dentist.

As an additionally fresh approach, the two authors of this volume have worked *completely independently,* thereby preserving the element of contradiction. When the reader encounters two conflicting versions of the same event in Russian history, he is encouraged to accept whichever one comes closest to his own impression (if any).

RUSSIA, ANYONE?

A Completely
Uncalled-for History
of the U.S.S.R.

Catherine the Great   I
at Everything

AT THE MAIN INTERSECTION OF THE OLD RUSSIA AND
Modern Russia stands Catherine the Great. A great
deal is known about Catherine, and what we don't know
we can feel free to make up.

The reason for this is that Catherine lived a very
full life. She was married but it didn't take. Her husband, Peter III, was hated by the Russian people because he failed to relate to the group. Catherine, on the
other hand, got along very well with the Russians, especially the men. She learned French, which helped
her to be even more popular (with Frenchmen), and
read widely, specializing in letters thrown through her
window.

Catherine initiated many projects of reform, none of
them applying to herself—a surefire way of becoming
memorable. In particular she drew up a new code of
laws because the old laws applied only to people who
could not afford to hire a horse. Catherine's laws were

to apply only to people who could not afford to hire a lawyer. A considerably larger group. But this democratic impulse was killed by a peasants' revolt, which Catherine took personally.

Catherine makes alterations to the Kremlin

It should be noted here that the history of Russia is very rich in peasant revolts. Russian czars did not feel that their palace looked lived in unless there was a mob of peasants storming the gates.

The reason that Russian peasants revolted so often, compared to other brands of peasants, was that·it was a way to work off hostility in a country where there was a scarcity of pro wrestling.

But Catherine considered this particular peasant revolt to be in bad taste. (She had learned manners from the French, among other things.) She therefore turned around and became a despot, concentrating on foreign affairs (Voltaire, Montesquieu and Diderot). Her husband, having succeeded to the throne, was murdered by a group of conspirators led by one of Catherine's Russian lovers trying to boost local enterprise.

This made Catherine the empress of Russia, which luckily fitted in with her plans. Her first act was to sit

Chattel Serfdom

on the serfs, by giving the nobles absolute power over everything that couldn't speak French. This was the era of the dreaded Don Cossacks, who rode into village after village and subjected the people to folk songs till they gave up.

Next Catherine put one of her lovers on the throne of Poland and had enough lovers left over to occupy the thrones of Prussia and Austria. She proved that imperialism can be fun. By taking over Alaska she had a throne for lovers who had turned cold.

Catherine's favorite lover was Potemkin, who also worked on a battleship that was later made into a motion picture. *Battleship Potemkin* is still popular with art theater groups that meet on Sundays, and therefore typifies the Russian tendency toward atheism.

Catherine contributed to the arts like no other Russian ruler, so that in the end she became glorious. Her correspondence with Voltaire gave Russian literature *prestige,* as well as helping to promote a postal system of daily delivery.

Peter the Great II
at Nearly Everything

Peter the Great founds St. Petersburg

CATHERINE'S SUCCESSOR, PAUL I, WAS HANDICAPPED NOT only by his mother's being glorious but also by the fact that he was demented. He took after his father in that he was murdered.

The reason that most of Russia's emperors were crazy was that they were too proud to marry outside the family. This led to inbreeding, which is contrary to proper respiration (breed in, breed out, breed in, breed out) and also affects the mind.

The long line of potty Peters and Pauls went back to Peter the Great, who took Russia out of the Middle Ages and after a long reign decided to put her back. Peter the Great organized the dreaded Cossacks and encouraged the sport of serf riding. He also introduced the Russian navy, though not to anybody worth knowing.

In order to make Russia look more Western the emperor forced the upper classes to wear pants and shave off their beards, thus causing the Russian church to be-

Peter the great
abolishes beards

come unorthodox. Peter simplified the fiscal system by keeping all the money for himself.

Finally, at banquets he popularized the Russian wolf-hound with his famous remark: "We have no napkins, but a woolly dog will pass among you."

Bringing Western civilization to Russia

By making all these reforms Peter the Great left the common people worse off than ever. This marked the beginning of modern government.

Alexander the Not So Great   III

ALEXANDER THE GREAT WAS ONE OF THE GREATEST MILI-
tary commanders the world has ever known, but Russia
got the wrong Alexander. The Russian Alexander got
into a war against Napoleon and saw that his best plan
was to get out of it. He therefore made peace with
Napoleon and annexed Finland instead. (Cf. old Russian saying: "When in doubt, annex Finland.")

Alexander's
Ragtime Band

Alexander also gained Bess Arabia (affectionately called "Good Queen Bess") as well as several territories

Tchaikovsky conducts his 1812 Overture

in the Caucasus that entitled the Russians to call themselves Caucasians and eat in any southern restaurant
they liked.

Napoleon then began his famous march on Moscow.
Alexander kept his military record intact by retreating
faster than the French could advance. He abandoned
Moscow to Napoleon in the middle of winter, leaving
Napoleon with nothing to do but go home to France

through blizzards and snowballs thrown at him by Russian ski bums. This expedition gave Russia a very poor reputation as a country to invade. The French were so disgusted that they made Russia an ally.

Moscow
Cookout

Nicholas I, IV
Definitely
Un/Great

Lessons in Citizenship (Under Nicholas)

UNDER NICHOLAS, RUSSIA BECAME KNOWN AS "THE policeman of Europe" because her development was arrested. Nicholas instituted a program of education for the peasants consisting of teaching them a lesson they would never forget. His foreign policy was to help

other countries put down *their* peasants. He commis-
sioned a designer to build a slower sled, for peasants
pursued by wolves.

Nicholas I, Definitely Un-Great

During this period Russia extended her relations with the Western powers by going to war against them over the Crimea. The main result of the Crimean War was a protective headgear called the Balalaika.

Also, the war made famous an English nurse called Flo Nightingale who formerly sang in Berkeley Square. Miss Nightingale revolutionized nursing by bringing a lamp into the operating room so that the doctors could see what they were amputating. She met strong opposition from doctors who could not stand the sight of blood.

Nurse Nightingale's insistence on sanitary arrangements ruined the Crimean War for everybody. The war dragged on, at considerable expense, till a member of the British House of Commons arose and said "Crimea does not pay."

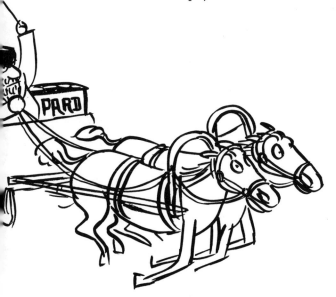

Also-Romanovs   V

ALEXANDER II FOLLOWED NICHOLAS I AS EMPEROR, BUT he proved to be liberal-minded and was therefore disqualified.

Alexander III was properly reactionary, instituting a soil program based on treating the peasants like dirt.

Construction of the Trans-Siberian railroad opened up Siberia for Russians who were dissatisfied with con-

ditions in other parts of the country. It became the only railway in the world that did not sell return fares. Family excursions to the salt mines were very popular with the czar, who found that he could save on food bills by putting people in the freezer.

To help him avoid progress Alexander had an adviser, Count Witte, who stimulated grain production by raising a riding crop.

Nicholas II—the End VI

NICHOLAS II WAS THE LAST OF THE CZARS THOUGH HE DID not know it at the time. The emperor had a reactionary entourage that saved him the trouble of personally concentrating on doing nothing. He was able to devote himself to moving from his summer palace to his winter palace and back to his summer palace without getting his seasons mixed up.

Russia abandoned the Three Emperors' League because Germany was getting the best players. With Britain and France she made a Triple Entendre that was even dirtier than a Double Entendre. The understanding was that if a country attacked one of them the other two would automatically become very annoyed, unless it was one of them.

Nicholas II was related by marriage and other things to the emperors of Germany, Austria, Britain, etc., all of whom wore a small beard and mustache, a field cap and the expression of trying to remember where they had left something.

The emperors liked to keep everything in the family, especially war. Russia and Japan went to war in 1904 because it was the only year still open. The czar hoped that the war would divert the peasants, who seemed to think of nothing but their stomachs while starving to death.

The Japanese failed to cooperate, however, attacking without a formal declaration of war, which automatically let Britain and France out. The Japanese seized Port Arthur and moved toward Fort William. They bottled up the Russian fleet, selling the bottled ships as souvenirs to tourists.

Sauce au Russe

Russia, Anyone?

The Russo-Japanese War was finally won by President Theodore Roosevelt, who moved the whole dispute to Portsmouth, N. H., and made both sides give up by carrying a big stick. This confused the Russian peasants so badly that they started the Revolution of 1905, which forced the czar to set up a parliament called the Duma and as a further precaution to take away all its powers (cf. old revolutionary song "How Come You Duma Like You Do, Do, Do?").

This period marked the rise of the proletariat, workers who wore cloth caps and braces though they had nothing to lose but their chains. The czar showed his impartiality by putting them down as hard as the peasants.

The premier, Stoolpin, tried to conciliate the peasants by breaking up the land and making them all landowners, which was all right till the peasants found out that it was their land that he was breaking up.

Russian foreign policy at this time was devoted to Pan-Slavism, according to which everybody in Europe was a Slav except Britons, who never, never will be Slavs. This resulted in the shooting of the Archduke Ferdinand, the Bull of Bosnia, by a Serbian Pan-Slaver. This became the shot that was heard round the world, thanks to the wireless telegraph.

Hard Cell

Soft Cell

Russia, Anyone?

World War I did not agree with Russia. The army had only one piece of equipment—the Russian steamroller. When this ran out of steam and started rolling backward, the army became demoralized and fraternized with the peasants.

To make matters worse the empress came under the influence of a dirty old monk named Rasputin who kept all the state secrets hidden in his beard. Rasputin had a strong magnetism that enabled him to cure women who were not even sick. His miraculous powers included the power to stop bleeding. Ministers who opposed his policies found out that there were certain kinds of bleeding that Rasputin did not stop.

Thanks to the empress, Rasputin got into the emperor's cabinet, and other home furnishings. This led a group of conspirators to poison Rasputin, but as it was not easy to make an amendment to his constitution, they also had to riddle him with bullets and drown him in the River Neva. He was later dug up and burned by a mob that shouted, "Better lit than Neva."

With Rasputin murdered, the army routed and the people in open revolt, Nicholas II sensed that trouble was brewing. He got off the throne but stayed around in case things improved enough for him to get on it again. This was a mistake, since the whole royal family was taken into a cellar from which only about twenty or thirty emerged alive, later moving to Paris, London and Hollywood with the title of Grand Duchess Anesthesia.

Rasputin-the power behind the throne

Let's run him up and see if anyone salutes

Lenin, and Other VII Communist Sympathizers

To understand the Russian Revolution it is necessary to go back to Karl Marx, or better still have somebody else go back. Marx was a professor of economics who got fired for instituting class warfare (somebody complained after being hit with a chalk eraser). He then wandered from one country of Europe to another working up bad feeling toward *capitalism*, a word he made up to explain why labor was such hard work.

Marx finally sat down in Switzerland and wrote *Das Kaput*, in which he described his theory of dietetical materialism, a fat-free philosophy for people who were not eating much anyhow.

The main part of Marx's system was the accordion, as expressed in his famous statement: "From each accordion to his ability; to each accordion to his needs." This appealed to the Russians, who were getting tired of hearing nothing but fiddles playing "Ochi Chorniye."

Marx taught that capitalism was responsible for everything that was wrong with the world with the possible exception of athlete's foot. With socialism the state

37

Marx studying in the British Museum

would wither away, he said, and everybody could buy anything they wanted, because there would be no postman to deliver the bills.

Marxism appealed to Lenin, a Russian who wanted to get even because nobody ever called him by his first name (Vladimir). His second name was Ilyich, which didn't help matters. His last name was Ulyanov. The history of the world was changed because at school a kid was called Ily Ulyanov.

To make things worse, his father was a school official. The family belonged to the minor gentry, which meant that little Ily had to have his photo taken wearing a tight sailor suit and holding an Easter lily.

Thanks to Marx, Lenin was able to blame all these hardships on capitalism. He therefore gave up the study of law and decided to become a full-time revolutionary, even though the profession was crowded and the government-approved retirement plan had its drawbacks.

Lessons in Citizenship (Planned Obsolescence)

Lenin, and Other Communist Sympathizers

By preaching revolution to the workers in St. Petersburg, Lenin won two expenses-paid trips to Siberia. This gave him enough status among the revolutionaries to organize his own group, called the Bolsheviks. The Bolsheviks were left-wing Marxists. They wanted to free not only the oppressed Russian worker but also the oppressed worker everywhere. Any worker that wasn't oppressed they would oppress for him and thus make him eligible.

When World War I broke out, Lenin volunteered for service in Switzerland. There he fired off a lot of writings to show that the war was a capitalist plot to develop a market for mud. Toward the end of the war, when the Russian army was reeling (its favorite maneuver), Lenin was sneaked back to Russia via Sweden in a sealed railway car, the introduction of the European package tourist plan.

By organizing the people to run into the city's open squares and get mowed down, Lenin's Bolsheviks gained control of the revolutionary government. Lenin seized the reins of government, but found there was no horse. Everything was in a mess owing to the Russians' not being English.

Lenin changed the name of the Bolsheviks to the Communist party and set up a council of commie-czars whose job was to make sure that whatever a person did there was no profit in it.

Mother Russia Gone Red   VIII

THE FIRST THING THE COMMUNIST GOVERNMENT DID WAS
to trade in the old war with Germany on a brand-new
war, called the war between the Reds and the Whites.
Lenin had the Reds, the generals had the Whites, and
the peasants, as usual, had the Blues (in the night).

Charge Now

Many of the White Russians had fled to become Paris taxicab drivers, and those that were not already white soon turned white.

Russia's civil war was fought mainly in the deep South—Georgia and the Urals (actually the Ur Mountains but people down there pronounced it *Ur-al*). Helping the Whites were armies from the Allies, who suddenly realized how much they were going to miss Nicholas II and his wholesome attitude toward private property. Around Russia the Allies set up the Cordon Sanitaire, a school of French chefs whose cooking would remind the Russians how hungry they were.

The Reds beat the Whites, however, by unfairly coordinating their forces. The Red responsible for this was the Fox Trotsky, a civilian whose military experience was unfortunately limited to winning. Trotsky

Pay Later

Introduction of the Five Year Plan

later promoted his own brand of Marxism, for export, but instead of its being exported, Trotsky was.

Lenin's other helper, Joseph Stalin, smoked a large, curved pipe till Lenin had a stroke and died. Stalin then took over the Soviet government and started the first Five Year Plan, which ran for ten years in accordance with the revised Russian calendar. The reason the Communists brought out a new calendar was that anybody found using the old czarist calendar could do time.

To keep his fellow Russians on their toes Stalin also modernized the secret police, putting them into long rubber trench coats and repotting the palms in restaurants, hotels, etc. Instead of being shot down in the

Trial Offer

open square the average Russian now enjoyed the luxury of being shot down in the comfort of his own living room.

The Soviet government kept control of the newspapers, but by raising the level of literacy it enabled millions of Russians to read what they were to think. This was a big improvement over the time when most Russians were so ignorant that they had to think for themselves.

The Communist program was sweeping. The men organized the program and the women did the sweeping. This kept the streets of Moscow clean of everything, especially people.

The peasants were organized into huge farms called collectives because whatever the farmers grew the state collected it. Some of the collectives were called kolkhozes and others sovkhozes, and if neither of these appealed to the peasant he had the option of going to one of the old-fashioned forced labor camps (bunkhozes).

Thanks to all this agrarian reform Russia had a famine. This famine differed from earlier, czarist famines in that formerly the poor starved whereas under the new regime *everybody* starved. The Communists therefore restored a bit of capitalism to the system by allowing the peasants to have a small vegetable plot for their own use. The next year these small plots accounted for

90 percent of total production. This annoyed the Soviet government, which decided to take out the bit of capitalism and try to get the peasants interested in free love instead. But free love never caught on like the private beds of vegetables.

Togetherness

Joe the Glorious   IX

JOSEPH STALIN WAS CALLED THE MAN OF STEEL BECAUSE
he invented the Iron Curtain. He became premier of
the U.S.S.R. by virtue of the fact that none of the other
leaders could tell what he was thinking till it was too
late.

Stalin introduced a new electoral system which entitled every Russian to cast a secret ballot on which all
the candidates belonged to the Communist party,
thereby eliminating a great deal of confusion and making it much easier to determine which party had won
the election.

The Communist party won 99.9 percent of the votes
in every election, the remaining .1 percent being ballots
spoiled by voters who mistook the ballot box for a
spittoon. To be on the safe side, Stalin began his famous
purges. He was responsible for so many purges that he
became known as the Enema of the People.

One reason why Stalin's purges were so successful in
getting rid of unsightly opponents to the regime was
that the Russian judicial system combined the more

efficient elements of British and Napoleonic law; that is, a person was judged to be guilty until he was proved to be guilty.

Lessons in Citizenship
(Under Stalin)

Before the trials the defendants were provided with special assistance that enabled them to make a full public confession of all the crimes they were charged with. Since many of them were Stalin's old revolutionary comrades, they thus refuted the decadent American saying "Even your best friends won't tell you."

After liquidating those Russians who showed opposi-
tionist tendencies, such as wearing a tie to dinner, Stalin
spent the next ten years watching the Red Army march
through the Red Square. On this occasion he was
flanked by top Soviet officials who looked as if they had
given up all hope of ever having their suits made in
Italy.

With the Russian satellite states of Poland, Hungary,
Rumania, etc., Stalin set up a trade program that con-
sisted of their sending Russia all their grain and receiv-
ing in return any number of large pictures of Stalin.
He also provided the satellites with a defense system
based on the idea that they were their own worst enemy.

Russia arranged to be left out of World War II, because she was only interested in war that had class. But
Hitler invaded Russia anyhow, having predicted a "six-
weeks' war," forgetting that the Russians had no sense
of time.

During the war Stalin met with Churchill and Roosevelt for the purpose of having their picture taken together. Russia came out best from these conferences because Stalin could not understand a word that was said.
He just kept smiling inscrutably until the other mem-
bers had talked themselves into Yalta, Potsdam and
other messes.

After the war Stalin surprised everyone by dying. Nobody had suspected that he had this human side to his nature.

Russia tested her first atomic bomb under Malenkov, but he had nothing for an encore. Also, Malenkov had a plump figure that did not go well with the grain shortage. He was succeeded by Bulganin, who had a small beard and did not go well with anything, particularly Khrushchev.

Introducing home recordings in Russia

Nikita the Jolly X

PREMIER KHRUSHCHEV THEREFORE TOOK OVER AND called for a summit meeting with Western leaders, and as soon as they had assembled in Paris he walked out. This showed his sense of humor. Khrushchev brought the language of diplomacy closer to the barnyard, which led France to develop her own atomic bomb.

Another thing Khrushchev did was to get up at the Soviet Congress, the annual meeting of delegates appointed to nod their heads from every part of Russia, and denounce Stalin as having been no better than he should have been. In particular he accused Stalin of having a personality, which was contrary to Marx, who taught that whoever was at the top should blend in with the rest and not be noticed unless he blew his nose.

Khrushchev's attack on Stalin resulted in the removal of Stalin's statue and picture from public places, a rewriting of history texts to deglorify Stalin, and a good deal of bad feeling in Stalin's home town (Stalingrad). It also upset Red China, which was just catching up with the revolution and whose history texts were a lot harder to rewrite because of all the squiggly lines.

Russia, Anyone?

Khrushchev was the first Russian premier to visit the United States. He was allowed to visit all parts of the country except that considered vital to U.S. security (Disneyland). The Americans put up with the Russians' stealing plans for nuclear bombs, but they were determined to retain exclusive possession of Donald Duck.

The Image Maker

The Russian premier toured Hollywood studios and watched dancing girls doing the cancan. He later described the dancing as immoral. He was with Mrs. Khrushchev at the time. It has been estimated that Khrushchev's denouncing the cancan cost the French Communist party two million votes in the subsequent election and made De Gaulle unassailable.

The Russian leader also visited the farmlands of the American Midwest. Chatting with the farmers in their fields, he proved that he could be very affable when standing someplace where it was wise to keep his shoe on.

Although unable to shake off that old bugbear, declining grain production, Khrushchev proved to be Russia's best premier at hugging and kissing. The hugging and kissing trade with China fell off around 1961, but Khrushchev made it up with hugging and kissing Cuba's Castro, Russian cosmonauts, American ambassadors' wives and so on.

Khrushchev thus brought Russian history full circle back to Catherine the Great, whose hugging and kissing put the country on the map.

Very Early Russia   XI

IT IS IMPOSSIBLE TO UNDERSTAND MODERN RUSSIA WITH-
out knowing something about Russia before Catherine
the Great. Since nothing is known about Russia before
Catherine the Great, this doesn't help much.

From Hollywood's reconstruction of the period we
know that while the rest of Europe was learning to use
a knife and fork, Russia was still being roamed by fierce
barbarian tribes wandering about in search of bosomy
girls having trouble with the upper part of their cos-
tumes.

These tribes were known as Scythians because they
were too primitive to use a power mower. They were
very good at orgies. The tribes took turns galloping up
and down the steppes, putting everybody to the sword
and/or torch. The fiercest of all were the Tartars,
creators of a sauce that subjugated the rest for some
time.

After several hundred years of being nomads, the
tribes of Russia gradually realized the advantage of
coming in out of the rain. They built the House of

Rurik, Rurik being a Swede (or Rus) who had some experience with living indoors. He proved this by having a dynasty.

Under the House of Rurik, Vladimir the Great got rid of his eight hundred wives by embracing the Church. This left him with one wife and made him a saint. To celebrate his death his sons murdered one another. This encouraged the warlike tribes to make a strong comeback, especially the Polovtzy nomads who became the subject of the Russian epic *Prince Igor's Band*. The Band played The Polovtzian Dances, which brought down the House (of Rurik).

Next Russia was overrun by the Mongrels, half Chinese and half cavalry. The Mongrels, also known as the Golden Herd, were led by Genghis Khan and his equally antisocial sons Astra Khan and Peli Khan. By defeating all the Russian armies they made Russia Oriental for hundreds of years, during which there was nothing new except gunpowder.

Also a large section of the Russian people became known as the Little Russians, having been lopped off at the knees.

However, the new town of Moscow produced a line of dukes who turned out to be grand. These grand dukes were all named Ivan and paid tribute to the Mongrels till the Mongrels started quarreling among themselves, upon which the current Ivan became Terrible.

Mongols initiate collective farming

Ivan the Terrible's full name was Ivan Petruski Skavar, and his most famous battle was against Abdul the Bulbul Amir, a fight that went on for thirty-three choruses.

Ivan's son having gone mad waiting, the state was ruled by his brother-in-law Boris Godunov. Little is known about Boris Godunov except that he was definitely not a tenor.

After the crazy czar died Boris was elected to the throne, but he never really caught on because it was widely believed that he had murdered Ivan's other son, Dmitri. People just stood around at Boris's parties, sniffing their drinks and looking uncomfortable.

Boris relieved everyone's mind by dying, but a swarm of false Dmitris settled on the throne as well as one Basil who got in by mistake. Since none of these impostors was a baritone, this period is known in Russian history as the Time of Treble.

Casting about for a czar that would keep, the Russians came up with the grand-nephew of the wife of Ivan IV, the Romanov family that strengthened the throne's tendency toward insanity. Under the first two Romanov czars the landlords were given new powers over runaway serfs, provided they could catch them. Also the Church discovered that it had been saying its prayers wrong. As a result of the reform, the Church fell into a schism. This left millions of Russians as Old Believers with no place to go on Sunday except out of their mind.

When Peter I was named czar his older half-sister Sophia succeeded in having her half-witted brother declared co-ruler, with herself as regent. She then tried to reduce Peter's work load further by having him assassinated, along with his mother. This feminine touch in

politics showed that Russia was becoming more West-
ernized. Sophia paved the way for

Catherine the Great XII
at Everything

THIS IS WHERE WE CAME IN.

Appendix—
Russian Art, Music and Like That

1. ART

Russian art has never really got off the ground, because the country is too cold to paint nudes.

Instead of painting nudes Russian painters painted icons, which were not suitable for framing. For hundreds of years they went on painting icons. Nobody told them about painting pictures. Also, the Church made it illegal to paint anything that would sell.

After the Revolution, Russian painters gave up painting icons and started painting the Revolution. Some painted a farm worker standing on a tractor urging the peasants to exceed their production quota. Others painted a factory worker standing on a slag heap urging the iron workers to exceed *their* production quota. But none of the painters got any closer to painting a nude, because nobody was urging the workers to get on with central heating.

Russia, Anyone?

Another reason why Russian artists have been backward is they have continued to use a brush and paints to paint with, instead of using a slingshot to fire gobs of axle grease at a canvas, then riding a bicycle over the goo. Most Russian artists do not own a bicycle. Russia is rocketing to the moon, but her artists still have to walk over their paintings.

Self portrait

2. MUSIC

Earliest forms of Russian music were folk songs, steppe-dancing, saber-rattling and "Dark Eyes," a ballad played by wandering gypsy violinists whenever they smelled food.

Russia, Anyone?

Best known of Russian popular songs is "The Song of the Vulgar Boatmen." The boatmen were called vulgar because they were so poor that they had no water for their boats and had to pull them overland.* They sang the song to let each other know how much they wished they were doing something else.

Because they worked to background music like this the peasants were called Muzaks.

* Cf. Russian squatting dance, developed by peasants who wanted to sit down but had no chair.

The Volga Boatmen

In serious music the Russians did very well during the Romantic period because they were Slavonic and naturally moody. Most famous of these was the composer who wrote symphonies for a lady he loved but was too bashful to speak to—Shy Kowski.

More contemporary Russian composers include Shostakovich, Khachaturian and other sneezes. Their music shows Marxist influence in that the brass have to work as hard as the other parts of the orchestra, and nobody gets to end up ahead.

Russia, Anyone?

Russian composers that copied the decadent American music, such as jazz, were taken to Task (in Siberia). Even so, in recent years Russian youth has shown a great interest in such Americana as rock 'n' roll and the twist, giving the West reason to hope that Communism has met its match in the teen-ager.

3. BALLET

The Russians have been good at ballet because they have had so much practice at having to express themselves without saying anything.

Famous Russian choreographers include Fokine, Diaghilev and Minsky, who brought to America such eminent dancers as Nijinsky, Karsavina and Cupcakes Cassidy. (Another great Russian vaudeville act was Pavlov and His Dogs.)

Best known of the Russian ballet companies is the Ballet Russe de Monte Carlo, where it popularized "Chemin de Fer," "Faites Vos Jeux," "Russian Roulette," and other well-known works. The only ballet company left in Russia is the rather old-fashioned Bolshevik Ballet, which is sold out night after night either because most Russians don't own a television set or because most Russians *do* own a television set.

Pavlov seeks world recognition

4. LITERATURE

Literature has been Russia's strong suit, artwise. Russian writers have written more great classics that people are going to read next summer for sure than any other country's writers.

Russia, Anyone?

Best known of the great Russian novelists are Tolstoi and Chekhov (in that order), their names being easier to pronounce than the other great Russian novelists (Dostoevski, Turgenev, *et al.*). One of these wrote the Brothers Karamazov but never got an answer. Such incidents made Russian writers rather glum, so that even in Russian comedies all the fun lies in watching the characters stagnate.

Stagnation is very big with Russian writers. They like to assemble a large group of characters, representing every level of society, and have them all stagnate together. By giving each character three or four different names they amass a truly staggering amount of vegetation.

Russia has had only one poet—Pushkin. Russians have not written much poetry because they have enough trouble without also suffering in translation.

5. ARCHITECTURE

All modern Russian buildings appear to have been designed by an architect who apprenticed with the birthday-cake department at Kresge's. The University of Moscow looks delicious.

6. EDUCATION

Russian schoolchildren are more politically conscious than those of the West, thanks to the fact that every time there is a change of government the textbooks are rewritten. When Russian students toast the premier's health, they mean till after the exams.

Russian universities turn out tremendous numbers of scientists and engineers. They do this by convincing women that they look good in a white smock and a tin hat. Russian universities are coeducational, but you have to take their word for it.

Russian coeds train to be physicists, sailors and dentists, but are very weak in baton twirling.

Anybody with sufficient intelligence and desire to learn can attend a Russian university, the state paying his tuition and a living allowance. On the other hand, there is no incentive to major in pantie raids. (Russian women's underwear does not progress beyond the elementary level.)

Russian teachers are in the highest salary bracket regardless of whether they are the team coach. As a result, no Russian university has ever won the academic distinction of playing in the Rose Bowl.

7. ECONOMICS

In recent years the U.S.S.R. has been adopting more and more of American methods of commerce. It is expected shortly to announce that Russia invented profits.

To stimulate the economy the Communist government has approved installment buying. In this way it has solved the leisure problem of Russians who had been just sitting around at the end of the month instead of opening bills and striking their foreheads with the palm of the hand. Time had hardly existed for a people that was not buying on it.

Instead of being enslaved by the state, the Russian people can now join in the do-it-yourself method long popular in North America.

Introduction of installment buying in the U.S.S.R. has meant the creation of a new job: the credit manager. These posts are being filled by MVD men who proved too brutal for regular police work.

If Ivan misses one of the payments on a purchase he receives a friendly reminder from the head of his local labor camp. The penalty for failing to keep up with the installments is much the same as in the West, except that instead of Ivan's losing the furniture, the furniture loses Ivan.

By this and similar modification of Marxist economic doctrine, Russia is moving closer to the free enterprise system. At the same time, the United States, with its expansion of the welfare state, is moving closer to socialism. Economists expect that somewhere around 1970 the two systems will pass one another—Russia moving to the right, the U.S. moving to the left—a phenomenon leading some observers to predict that the choice of next premier of the U.S.S.R. will be a tossup between Mikoyan and Barry Goldwater.

8. SCIENCE

The Russians were the first to fire into orbit a man in a space capsule, proving how anxious the Russian is to have a room of his own.

The Soviet government gives its citizens every encouragement to travel, as long as it is to a different planet.

Russian science is ahead of the world in such things as space rockets, atomic weapons and modern fishing trawlers, but lags badly in the development of an electric toothbrush, pastel shades of telephone and underarm deodorants.

9. OTHER PASTIMES

Russians must know about sex since the population is over two hundred million. But there is no other way of telling. Apparently it has caught on as a result of word-of-mouth.

There is hardly any sex in Russian novels, films and magazines. Russian ballerinas are not considered ripe till over forty. And while it is true that Soviet women wear very skimpy bikinis at the seaside, it is difficult

to know whether this represents sex appeal or a crisis in Russia's textile industry.

As a result, Russian social life gives the general impression of having been organized by the Brownies. The only place where Russians get excited about mating is on the chessboard.

In television programs, the Russians are so far behind the U.S. that if people get sick they have to go to a doctor. Instead of watching TV, Russians do a lot of reading, with the result that their children grow up without any real understanding of the judo chop, the Three Stooges, or how to fall, riddled with arrows, under a moving train without hurting themselves.

CONCLUSION

The trouble with Russia is that she arrived in history late and caused an awful disturbance finding her seat. It might be better if she went out and came in again.

The only thing wrong with the Russian people is that they haven't learned that the only thing worse than not having what they want is getting what they want. It is their kind of attitude that gives innocence a bad name. They would be easier to get along with if they shared with Western peoples the deep and sincere conviction that the future belongs to crab grass.

Russia, Anyone?

Russians' brotherly regard for each other has survived because not enough of them yet own cars to compete for parking space.

Our best hope for peace is that soon Russian society will be so affluent that the Communists will have to forget about world revolution in order to find out why the automatic washer is going thumpity-thumpity.

It's either them or us, and it had better be both.

RUSSIA TOMORROW —

The 51ST, 52ND, 53RD, 54TH, 55TH, 56TH, 57TH, 58TH, 59TH, 60TH, 61ST, 62ND, 63RD, 64TH, 65TH STATES?

75

WAY OF LIFE

MAY DAY PARADE

ORDER OF
THE
DAUGHTERS
OF THE OCTOBER
REVOLUTION

INDUSTRY

THE ARTS

CANDID CAMERA

EYE WITNESS

HAVE BOMB

WILL TRAVEL

I'VE GOT A SECRET

RED CHORUS SING ALONG

AND SCIENCES

INSTITUTE FOR RESEARCH ON FERTILITY

POLITICS

Bibliography

Junior Book of Knowledge, vol. 8 (RUBE-SPIT), 1898, etc.

15 Different Things To Do with Vodka, Esquire Press, 1962.

I Am Eagle! by Harry Eagle (privately printed).

What Outer Mongolia Means to Me, by V. M. Molotov, Fibber & Fibber, 1961.

Dick and Jane in the Kremlin, Communist Youth Books, 1959.